THE SMELL OF
SAGE AND CEDAR

THE SMELL OF SAGE AND CEDAR

CAREY TACHEENE

Library of Congress Control Number:		2020911971
ISBN:	Hardcover	978-1-9845-8549-3
	Softcover	978-1-9845-8548-6
	eBook	978-1-9845-8547-9

Print information available on the last page.

Rev. date: 06/25/2020

To order additional copies of this book, contact:
Xlibris
1-888-795-4274
www.Xlibris.com
Orders@Xlibris.com
815942

CONTENTS

The Smell of sage and cedar

Do you remember the smell of sage and cedar?
White wool and blue corn mush on a brown table
The way she would hold me tight in her arms
And pray to the gods
This was my mother
Navajo words so gentle and pure
The touch of her hand
Her heart is so warm
The love that she showed
The smell of her clothes
The smell of the hearth juniper cedar
This was grandmother
Arizona air smells of sage and cedar
The smell of my home and where my heart is
I recognize the bittersweet smell of cedar earthy and soulful
The sage smells salty and savory
Such a mystical and magical satisfaction
This is my mother earth
Each deep breath fills me with home
I love the smell of sage and cedar
In the spring
In the summer, in the fall
In the winter is the smell of sage and cedar

Whispers the wind

Why the sadness whispers the wind?

I am your friend

The bringer

The giver, the one who has seen the world

I am your friend that helps lift your wings

Pretend to fly with me whispers the wind

Forget your worries whispers the wind

Breathe me in whispers the wind

I am the bringer

I bring you beauty renewal flowers sweet fragrance of spring

Why the sadness whispers the wind?

Lay your troubles down for me

I may take them away with me

I may carry them far away whispers the wind

Atop this hill I stand today

Why the sadness whispers the wind?

Soulful

Verse 1 check, check
Notes so smooth like velvet things
Subtle hints do these words sure bring
La la, la, sing the words to me
Shake and shimmy my whole body
In and out and down I go

Mic 1 mic check
I follow the sounds to and froe
Strings and horns oh my oh my
Notes so smooth like velvet things
Subtle hints do these words sure bring
Listen, an elusive chanteuse she sings
Soulful sweet serenity
Soulful hints of all of me

Fade away uncertainty
Music is my soulful medicine
Mic check mic 1 check, check

Broken to pieces

Marks of scrapes from kitchen knives
Chop these and those onions and chives
Visits from teapots sweet with sugar cubes
Talks of gossip
Confessions of love
Dreams of muses
Savory smells of soups and beans
Occasional oops I dropped a little teacup
Like my life it has broken to pieces
Pieces and pieces
Call the broom
Swift and nifty
Clean, clean, clean
Now it seems to me as I gaze upon my table
It has seen
Occasional oops I dropped a little teacup
Like my life it has broken to pieces
Pieces and pieces
What broken to pieces has your kitchen table ever seen?

Rainbows and cupcakes

Raindrops of rainbow
Colorful sprinkles
Atop clouds of whipped cream
Sweet fluffy cake
Rainbows and cupcakes
Paired with aromatic black coffee
Or sweet, sweet fruit punch
Sweet treats for me
My favorite is yummy white chocolate mousse
Rainbows and cupcakes
Paired with hazelnut cream
Mixed with black coffee for me
Hope no one minds but the kitchens a mess
Rainbows and cupcakes up the walls and everywhere

Silence sings the dark

Silence sings the dark
Silence she breaks my heart
Black is the widow bite
Poison the streams of will and might
Lost is my soul, so I weep
Fear caresses my essence my wish to be free
Labyrinth oh labyrinth
Be kind to me
In places unknown
Prison of invisible walls like quicksand I do sink
Though do I lay lifeless within a blanket of fear
Come hither
Release into me
I scratch and wince
I pray and I cry
I fight and I fight
Here do I lie
Invisible to all
Silence sings the dark
Lost in the weaves of this place
As silence sings the dark

Tribulations

As I close my eyes
Tears from inside cut like scattered glass
Into my hands my heart bleeds for what seems like an eternity
My thoughts exposed
Every ember of my soul
Is weak and brittle like a withered old rose
My breath is as weak
As I take ragged inhalations
I am vulnerable
Why is this my life?
Why is this who I am?
Where do I begin?
Here in my mind
I float in make believe
Clouds of reverie
Fervid is the sweet fantasy I pretend is so attainable
As I cry, I return to me, the me sitting in the room
Gloom filled and ominous
This room is a box, I am here in this box all alone and afraid
Halfway between dreams and blatant nightmares
These are thoughts from the pain that exist
In every fiber of me and my being my religions
my trials me and my tribulations

Teddy bear

Nobody
Nobody knows
If I tell him a secret
A secret only he knows
His name is Hairy
He's the sweetest
The sweetest to me
He holds my heart it says "please give me hugs"
Black buttons for eyes
A cute little nose
Hairy so innocent
Saw the painful tears that I've cried
Holds secrets for me
He's seen that I lied
And cheated at life
I held him so tight
Many a night
I cried and I cried
I held him so tight
Day after day
He's right by my side
Hairy is just for me
To you he is just another teddy bear
To me he is my might!

Yellow Rose Ranch

Yellow Rose Ranch
Red rocks reach to the sky, table top mesas
My childhood playground, where I roamed free
Danger, danger, danger, I never feared danger
Out there I dreamed I followed the sheep
grape Basha's Shasta and crackers
Grandmother would say
Connect with the earth
Connect with the sky
Follow the ants
Smell of the air
Yellow Rose Ranch Oh I Remember
The sound of summer cicada buzzing so loud and the humming so soft
Summer adventures me and my brother thicker than thieves
Running amuck pirates and power rangers and thunderous clouds
Sand in our shoes
The horizon ahead
Yellow Rose Ranch OH I remember
A Sheep corral oh that pungent sharp smell
and the feeling of soft lamb hair
Horses and cows, salt blocks and water troughs pretending
to be nothing could matter we didn't care
Climbing the rocks scaling the walls hiking down cliffs we were a pair
Collecting the sweet prickly pear berries and having a feast
So many memories from the adventures on Yellow Rose Ranch

Pieces to a million

How many pieces to a million?
A million to what?
A million to one
I wouldn't know
This a mystery I wouldn't know
How many pieces to a million? A million to what?
Piece by piece I built my heart
Piece by piece I built this army of one
One has my heart
One guards my soul
One gives me praise
Another fights the pain
Each one I would lay my life down for
How many pieces to a million? A million to what?
So many layers inside my brain
This ones for hurt
This ones for pain
This one remembers
This one forgets
This one is cold
This one regrets
I feel alive I feel like life
How many pieces to a million?
A million to what?
A million pieces of me inside my head shattered like glass
my heart is one in a million of many pieces to a million

There once was a cricket who lived in my shoe

There once was a cricket who lived in my shoe
Yes, this is true
I tried and I tried
I said shoo, shoo, shoo
He didn't move he didn't budge he hid in my shoe
He fiddles his play with his legs
It made no sense, no not even at all
There once was a cricket who lived in my shoe
Oh yes sir, its true
Before he gets crushed
Ill set him free
It seemed like forever he lived in my shoe
Only ten minutes I've spent with you
So, I cupped him in both of my hands
Out the front and away to a bush
I set him free oh yes, I did
And that dear sir is the story oh yes! Indeed
There once was a cricket who lived in my shoe

Ambiguous

I once was a child who dreamed of a love
Dashing white horse, valiant and bold
He would come to, and rescue me
I once was a child invisible in sight
I once was a child
With love in my alien heart
A loved left to turn blood into wine
Tossed aside like junk you don't need
Burned like scrap pieces of would
Cold and alone, I grew up on my own
Living and loving, what was that?
I was fierce with hate deep in my soul
The world wasn't ready for me to behold
It wasn't my fault I didn't know
I blamed it on you I blamed it on her
I made sure that you were the one
The cause of my pain, bear with me
The fight had begun
Like a roller coaster of filth and disease and
turns and breaks in the tracks
I mad a path more deadly than that
Here in my pain I lay still and awake
Tossing and turning because I had a pleasant and beautiful dream
Calm ad tranquil and nor narcissistic and all
I was outcast a shadow at that I space in the dark so ambiguous

Untitled

Why do I sit, and why do I cry?

Why do I stand and not lie?

Why do I crawl with good legs?

Why do I drag myself through these trenches of my own bloodshed?

When I hurt, I just cry I can't speak I can't say

In the mirror I see a fool deep in me a coward you see

I see my own worst enemy

When I hurt, I just cry I can't speak I can't say

I riddle my good deeds I destroy the heart seeds

I blind fold my hero I murder him too

I bathe my good name in ego and strife

Wickedly I laugh I chuckle, and I smile

I create this dark world

I hail to the sky

I dance in the rain

I feel so insane

I lost my old brain

I am the unsung hero for the monsters I have slayed

You look at me now

And pity for me so

"Are you alright? Are you okay?"

"Man up! Your punk, you're a wuss"

Don't take it lying down this is not why I opened to you all the book of black secrets a cradle of filth

I lay down my name I lay down my shame

Every night and everyday

I pray and I pray

What I wouldn't give for them second chances

I lived my life I lived my life

Don't believe in strife praying to God every night

Hearing me cry I miss who I used to be

Evil and smoke inside my head

There whispering things I don't want to hear
Living in this me God and bull shit
Love triangle
Living in this me God and bull shit
Love triangle
Holler at me if you need that love
You definitely...... need that love
And you ask me
Why I sit
And why I cry
These are the ingredients of what makes up my self-demise
The worst is over it's the toxic thoughts I despise
Therefore, I sit, and therefore I cry
Living in this ne God and bullshit
Love triangle

Arizona Summer Skies

OH, majestic Arizona summer skies
If I left, I'd ask myself why?
Your peaceful steady days
Your windy kicking up dust Saturdays
Red earth and pine tops too
Your saguaros tall and strong
Roadkill and western skies
But those Arizona sunsets oh my oh my
You haven't seen that beauty
Until you seen it in this Arizona sky
The pinks and purples orange and yellows
Majestic streaks strewn across my sky
The reds and blues the everything
Hazy lazy summer evening skies
The days are hot oh yes, they are
The red old echo cliffs
Grand Canyon on she beautiful take some pics
Arizona loves to shine when monsoon season is on the rise
The thunder and lightning make the earth a show
Theatrical and powerful come and see
I've always loved
My Arizona Summer Skies

DReAms

A multitude of vibrant colors
Etching like a majestic rainbow, after the storm
Boundless, breathtaking, celestial…. Imagination

Rainbows
Soft like my mama's touch
Warm like springs fresh air, rain drops capture light
Endless, mysterious, angelic I see the rainbow

My favorite flower
Soft and velveteen maroons
Brilliantly carved soft edges, blooming beautifully
Passion, subtle, subdued, petals of envious luxury

The Rain comes down

If I could find my way back to your heart
Now that I know
If I can think back when
I gave you my all
Now that I have learned
Leave no words left unspoken
Don't you fear all the danger and the lightning
strikes, but it never strikes the same
Or the same place twice
The rain comes down rivers run free the skies were blue
Now I color them gray, I mend my pain
The rain comes down and I cry my tears
The pain goes away, the rain comes down, the rain comes down
Time please wait time to waste
This time don't hesitate, don't hold back
Lead with your heart, even if it hurts
Turn back time, way back when
When you were mine
Before I tried to end it all

I gave you me I gave you love

I offered you my happiness
Wounds still fresh scar tissue and all
I placed it in your hands, sacred
Like a sacrifice
Dare I see you cry
Like a knight with armor shimmering in the sun
And a shield I would use to deflect the evil
And a sword made of faith
Into the fray I vow to protect your heart with courage and valor
I comment my being to protect your soul
Shield held high ill protect your life
Ill feel no pain ill heal your wounds
It's only fair, I promised you the world
Then I turned my cheek
And you walked away
I never want to fall in love again
The way it butchered me down to my last fibers
I'd lay my life down
Like prey poisoned in a web full of spiders
I gave you me, I gave you my all
Ever true, Ever thine
I gave you me, I gave you my all
With greed you took these things from me and
I envy you for you broke my heart

Just believe

If I just believe I believe I could do anything
I could fly, I wouldn't cry
I'd be an astronaut and circle the globe
I'd be a politician and right all the wrongs
Id be a scientist and find all the cures
I'd be Indiana jones and find the lost treasure
If I just believe I could do anything

       If I just believe
       I'd close my eyes
       I'd just pretend
       All the bad things were gone and far out of sight
       And you wouldn't hurt me not even at all
       You'd love me a lot
       And believe in my dreams
       If I just believe I can do anything

If I just believe I believe I can do anything
I could fly, I wouldn't have to cry
Id live in a mansion not in the ghetto
Id eat all my food and afford it all too
Id get a good job and pay all my bills
Id sacrifice dreams to raise all my seeds
Id lift my self up and walk once again
If I just believe it would hurt no one not even me
The paradox is it hurts me just to believe

Dreamcatcher

Call me collector
Call me dreamcatcher
I catch all these dreams
I see what could be
Every little possibility
Call me collector
Call me dreamcatcher
This is the story of how
I catch these feelings and even a vow
I look in your eyes
And see hope is so frail
I trusted you now
And you hurt me I collected the hurt
And locked it away
I kissed my goodbyes and laid them to rest
A prisoner for now
A blanket of evil
I cover my eyes
Call me collector
Call me dreamcatcher
Fairytales make believe
I live happily

When I fell in love with you

When I fell in love with you
I prayed I wish I hoped I dreamed
When I looked into your eyes
You met the love-struck teenager who believed in fairytales
Waiting for an everlasting love
Those soft eyes
Pools of dark mystery
In an instant I was afraid
Afraid of losing you
Afraid of wanting you
When I fell in love with you
I cried I sang I rejoiced I was scared
I felt your touch it was the thing that was missing in my heart
You reached into my soul
And found the me hiding in the shadows
Unafraid and destined to beloved
In that moment I seemed to glow

My eyes have seen my world crumble at my feet   I miss you still
Like a withered rose dried with time
I hide behind red moist eyes swollen and tender from the hours spent
While I cried
I feel a heaviness upon my shoulders
My heart weighs a million tons
The air I breathe constricts my life like hands wrapped around my neck
I feel the squeeze
My breathing slows
My mind knows I hear these voices whisper things to me
Gray colors the sky as I as I fall upon my knees
Loss is strewn across my mind
How I feel I can't compare to pain not felt before
Pictures scattered like faded glitter on the floor yet empty dark and ominous
My finger tips caress the edge of a picture I once knew and there was a
feeling I met once upon a time
A glimmer of a moment fading away hither too and froe
A sign of the happiness we once shared
I see your smile as you say I'll never leave
I'll never hurt you, you can always count on me
A single tear rolls down my face
As a fire sets of my sense and burns my nose as showers of liquid pour
down my face
Hugging the photograph, I lean back my head and scream out into the
unknown
My fingers find the opposite ends and I take a breath and with rage I rip
this piece in half
No one knows my pain, but everyone feels this pain
I collapse and exhale as the venom fills the air
My thoughts like tidal waves crashing into paradise unashamed of its
destruction
Silence
Silence pounds the sounds out until I hear nothing but my heart beat, I
miss you still

Imperfect Perfection Perfect Imperfection

My hair ain't all that I for damn sure am not the hottest in the room
My eyes are not sexy, and my face is too wide, am I doomed
My body needs work a nip and a tuck, who says? Everybody cares, this
is important stuff
My waist is not slim, I am not a 24, by far I am a 2
I wish my lips were plump to make a cute pouty face
The men don't look my way
They don't fall at my feet
But I am and will always be me, in my eyes I'm beautiful in my soul I'm
beautiful
I will not be defined by the lines drawn vogue will not be the epitome of
my life
I can throw anything on and look and feel fabulous
Wear my hair up or down
Messy buns I don't care
My smiles fine my teeth are crooked
But I am and will always be me, in my eyes I'm beautiful in my soul I'm
beautiful
I will not be defined by lines drawn
I'm not skinny I'm not fat
I'm not pretty and I ain't whack
My words is sometimes slick
I've learned to love the backwards me
My eyes are perfect my hair is beautiful my body is impeccable
I love the imperfect perfection to the broken pieces the lead to perfect
imperfection
I hold my head up high
I love myself I define imperfect perfection
I love myself I define perfect imperfection
Completely incomplete
These are the beautiful broken pieces that make me beautiful Carey

Medusa

Kneel before me
I'm more than your queen
I'm more than your future
Shower me in pearls
Feed me diamonds
Drape me in couture
I'm dangerous poison
Delicious heart
Rose petals for me to walk
Trumpets of triumph
Goddess of love
Now worship me
I'm the goddess of love
Raise your hand
Look too the sky
Hope for love
Peace on earth
The goddess is me
Worship me
Give me love
Or I may feed you to the medusa in me
This is honey
I'll be like medusa and have you falling in love with me
Just to clown
Strip you
And leave you a former realm of yourself, you were made to kneel at my embrace
Ill turn your love to ice cold stone I am medusa your goddess, now worship m

Struggle

There aint nothing I wouldn't give up for them second chances
For them second chances
Hood life had don't justify my life
Trap life had me married to the game love traded out for the fame
Forsaking my name everyone of all but me get that blame
Me living surviving hanging my down in shame
If you're living in the struggle know that I've been the same
Everybody in the street round the way know my name
Yeah, they know honey
Drink and smoke and evil in my head
I am living
I am Ballin' on a budget, I am stripping for my money
Corner liquor store is where you'll find me, I would be drinking every night
I am in them streets
Ill always be a winner, you will never see me at the bottom of the barrel
I am not a quitter, I got to keep it one hundred percent
I am always truthful
I am always beautiful
And I am always youthful
I better be keeping it in that party mode
I try to keep it peaceful
I'm LGBT I am keeping it simple
No hate and equality are all I want in this life
No struggle, no pain is all I want in this life
This is my struggle what's yours?

Touch me

I get Chills down every inch of my spine
My body starts ignites with passion
As my soul starts to rise in excitement
Touch me......
I close my eyes and I can feel every soft and tender sensation
As you caress my intimate skin
Touch me......
My heart begins to race
Racing against a backwards clock
From one hundred
My breath hastens
He desires me......
Touch me......
Wrap me up in your loving embrace
Warm my body
I long to touch you lips with my velvet lips
Face to face
I begin to feel like butterflies' flutter over my body
And a rush comes over me
Touch me.....

I am a "Fighter"

Though they have tried, succeeded not, they could not break my spirit
I closed the door the locked door, and destroyed he key
I'm not afraid for my life, I'm afraid for my heart
Please don't mistake me
It seems to you that from the outside underneath my skin
I hide and nurture innocent fears
No, they will never know the real me
I tried to stay along the path
That lead to good and just
I strayed away, and darkness followed offering intimacy
I embraced the wrath of the Devils' touch
Its too late to turn back now
They will never know the real me
The me inside used to be happy
These evil thoughts were like a drowning pool
And I kept slipping away
A shimmering ray of hope caught my eye
And I strayed away
Embraced the wrath of loves warm touch
As I search my soul, and journey to a treasure trove of answers
My strength I spent my mind is tattered my heart is beaten
My body lay damaged my soul is in need of mending
I've broken down the walls of my imprisonment
Now they will know the real me
I am a fighter

I am Triumph

Never have I not known triumph
My dear friend at every battle
Who's post and loyalty has forever more been by my side
We have seen a thousand wars
An army of me, the finest soldiers
At the forefront, there I stand, courage shines
around me like the sun brilliant and noble
I am triumph
In heroic blossom my hand strongly grips my weapons a sword of honor
Blood stained and golden from battle
I stand before my tribulations and look down
my nose at its pathetic destitution
I have come to slay the mighty beast
That plagues my soul
And I have conquered
I returned to my kingdom a hero of my domain
Never have I not know triumph
My dear friend in every battle
I am triumph

The plague of my temptations

I weep at the feet of my enemy
So that he will not fear me
I prey upon the valiant
My soul is wrought with disease, weak and hunger stricken
What lowly morsels of delight to feed upon?
He hearts of will
So, I disguise my intrigues with magical powers, a witch's brew
And so, the plague of my temptations unfolds before my blind eyes
"kindness" whispers the gentle intoxicating wind
"I see that you are Tired"
There is no darkness where you can see me"
"Come lay your weary troubles down" chants the nothing
I take comfort in her play, rue that she may ravage my soul
Damned is my doom
Reluctantly I quenched the thirst
As only she could feed and nurture me
The emptiness left behind like a motherless child
She is mother now
The plague of my temptations

Untitled

The rain fell upon me
My eyes were tired
My tears were dried up
I wept for days
And endless nights
Seconds seemed to go on forever
Promises of a better tomorrow overshadowed hope
A wise man once said "you eat shit then you die"
I have no words to live by but my own
The rain fell upon me
My eyes were tired
My tears were dried up
I wept for days
And endless nights

I've seen you here before

I've seen you here before
Your beauty has been spent
Years, days, minutes time has come and went
Only to leave me with the façade of being lonely and unwanted
I am the sunshine
A rainbow on a Thursday afternoon
The storms are far off in the distance
I was weak
I was strong
I did fight
One day my broken wings will heal
I will learn to fly once more
More than who I am today
And less then how I hurt before
I've seen you here before

A soul divided (Invisible)

I look up at a damaged window
Hopelessly devoted
To this emptiness I am feeling
Sometimes I feel that I am a prisoner of my own dreaming
Caged in a realm
Far beyond reach
Somewhere there hidden
Deep inside my soul
I am a scared little child since I was four
Relinquishing into a soul divided
I would always pray that I get an answer from up above
I don't know the words to say
To ask the questions
This is not the live I should have been given
I feel like I am not even in existence
I am invisible
Relinquishing into a soul divided
Something changed
I felt the universe in a moment
It spoke to me and asked me to lay my fears down in front of me
And all the strength they had stolen
Came back to me
And so I stand up and feel the light grow inside of me
I reach into the air, I reach up to the edge of that damaged window
My journey begins with a one question
Why do I keep relinquishing to a soul divided?

I'll be okay

I open my eyes to the sound of quiet
I am quietly breathing
Light cascades through the window curtains
My thoughts have been crashing in and receding back into the seas of
my mind
In all the moments in my life
Each dark thought befell me
The tempests have come and gone
I open my eyes to the sound of my voice
I'm saying ill be okay

CPSIA information can be obtained
at www.ICGtesting.com
Printed in the USA
BVHW030552150222
629065BV00005B/28

9 781984 585486